Poetry

Do Buses Eat Kids?

Poems about School

by Laura Purdie Salas

Capstone press
Mankato, Minnesota

Do Buses Eat Kids?

Hulking monster
Huge machine
Yellow jacket,
gleaming clean

Mirrors, metal
buttons, lights
Not sure if it
plays or bites

Slides up closer
Grins real wide
Asks me if I
want a ride

3

Ordinary

Pencil

Black tube hiding

Inside yellow wrapping

Leaves a trail of letters, stories,

Magic

Letters,
march across the lines
like soldiers

Watch out!
Don't tip over!
Stand tall,
no wiggling,
no leaning,
no shoving each other

You are my only
chance for a perfect grade
So you will make
a perfect line
even if I have to
march you
all day long

Stand Up Straight!

Mine

Little white numbers

Open my treasure

Chest that

Keeps

Each book, pencil, and secret note

Ready just for me

7

Friend Quiz

My best friend in the world is you

So you should know which things are true

What's my favorite color?
Blue as the sky in September?
Green as the grass Daddy mows?
Purple like lilacs that bloom in the spring?
Or silver like when the moon glows?

What's my favorite subject?
Math, for counting up numbers?
Reading, for stories and words?
Music, for singing and whistling tunes?
Or science, for coloring birds?

Who's my best friend?
The girl who lent me her sneakers?
Who called me when I had the flu?
Who likes to make lizards from sparkling beads?
Wait! All of these people are you!

Make It Up

Mountains, apple trees,

Snowflakes, dolphins, stormy seas. . .

All inside my brush

Tick Tock

tick-
    tock

watch the clock
minute-master of the day

tick-
    tock

bossy clock
always says we have to stay

tick-
    tock

slooooooooooooow clock
can't you move a faster way?

tick-
    tock

please, clock
tell us that it's time to play

What's for Lunch?

What's that?

I can't tell. . .

A barbecued beet?

Or jelly on eggs?

Or candy with meat?

Is it mustard on crackers?

Or ketchup on toast?

Or fries dipped in chocolate?

I love that the most!

Darn! It's nothing exciting

I'm sorry to say. . .

Dad must have packed lunches —

It's a ham sandwich day

16

MeMeMe

Pick me! Pick me! Pick me! Pleeeeeeeeaaaaase

I'm waving my arm
And knocking my knees

Pick me! Pick me! Give me a chance!

I'm doing my "I know
this answer" dance

Pick me! Pick me! Pick me! Now!

This one's easy
And I'll show you how

I did it! I did it! I gave it my best
Now my arm is exhausted, and I need to rest!

17

Take Your Best Shot

It's me against a sea of kids
That's how it looks from here
He's dribbling fast, or will he pass?
I have to show no fear

I'm guardian of this patch of grass
Defender of this goal
My chest is tight, I'm waiting now
The game's in my control

He boots it hard! I dive and grab —
Shot blocked! I don't know how!
I send it sailing down the field
Our goal is safe — for now!

A Helpful Tip

The secret solution is pink

It fizzes and makes people shrink

If I hand you a glass

Say, "No thanks, I'll pass,"

Or you'll disappear quick as a wink

20

Old Student

The school year lasts forever!

It's endless dying days

What's this plus that, the teachers ask,

and what makes up a phrase?

What? Learning lasts a lifetime?

Oh no — I hope you're wrong!

Just take a peek at Mr. Bones —

Don't make me stay that long!

Oh, Did You Need That Homework?

I've crunched your numbers
torn them up
'cause I'm a homework-
chomping pup

Thanks for leaving
out your pack
Your problems made a
tasty snack

Do them over
Such a shame —

But I'm just way
too cute to blame!

Finding My Place

Where will I go?

Who will I be?

How will I get there?

What will I see?

Will I go far?

Explore foreign lands?

I get to choose —

The world's in my hands.

Boring Bus Ride

Jeffrey's juggling apples
Lataya pens a note
Carlos croaks and ribbits
A frog's trapped in his throat

Driver hollers, "Quiet!"
Alexis sniffs her sock
The back row's playing hand games —
Paper smothers rock

Katie's playing trumpet
Jackson pokes Jerome
Another day on 88
Another bus ride home

The Language of Poetry

Couplet — two lines that end with words that rhyme

Repetition — the use of a word or phrase more than one time

Rhyme — to have an end sound that is the same as the end sound of another word

Rhythm — the pattern of beats in a poem

Acrostic

The subject of the poem is written straight down the page. Each line of the poem starts with one letter from the word. "Mine" (page 6) is an example of an acrostic poem.

Cinquain

A poem with five lines. The first line has two syllables. The second line has four, the third has six, the fourth has eight, and the last line has two syllables. "Ordinary" (page 4) is an example of a cinquain.

Free Verse

A poem that does not follow a set pattern or rhythm. It often does not rhyme. "Stand Up Straight!" (page 5) is an example of free verse.

29

Haiku

A short poem that describes a scene in nature. It has five syllables in the first line, seven syllables in the second line, and five syllables in the third line. "Make It Up" (page 10) is an example of a haiku.

Limerick

A five line poem that follows a certain rhythm. The first, second, and fifth lines rhyme, and so do the third and fourth lines. "A Helpful Tip" (page 20) is an example of a limerick.

Glossary

barbecue (BAR-buh-kyoo) — to cook over a grill

defender (di-FEND-uhr) — someone who protects something from harm

exhausted (eg-SAW-sted) — very tired

fizz (FIZ) — to bubble and hiss

foreign (FOR-uhn) — to do with or coming from another country

gleam (GLEEM) — to shine

guardian (GAR-dee-uhn) — someone who carefully watches and protects something

hulking (HUHLK-ing) — large and heavy

phrase (FRAZE) — a group of words that have a meaning but do not form a sentence

smother (SMUTH-ur) — to cover something

solution (suh-LOO-shuhn) — a liquid with something that has been dissolved in it

Read More

Barbe, Walter B. *A School Year of Poems: 180 Favorites from Highlights*. Honesdale, Penn.: Boyds Mills Press, 2005.

Hopkins, Lee Bennett. *School Supplies: A Book of Poems*. New York: Aladdin, 2000.

Internet Sites

Facthound offers a safe, fun way to find Internet sites related to this book. All of the sites on FactHound have been researched by our staff.

Here's how:

1. Visit *www.facthound.com*

2. Choose your grade level.

3. Type in this book ID **1429612061** for age-appropriate sites. You may also browse subjects by clicking on letters, or by clicking on pictures and words.

4. Click on the **Fetch It** button.

FactHound will fetch the best sites for you!

Index of Poems

A+ Books are published by Capstone Press,
151 Good Counsel Drive, P.O. Box 669, Mankato, Minnesota 56002.
www.capstonepress.com

1 2 3 4 5 6 13 12 11 10 09 08

Library of Congress Cataloging-in-Publication Data
Salas, Laura Purdie.
   Do Buses Eat Kids?: poems about school / by Laura Purdie Salas.
   p. cm. — (A+ books. Poetry)
   Summary: "A collection of original, school-themed poetry for children accompanied by striking photos. The book demonstrates a variety of common poetic forms and defines poetic devices" — Provided by publisher.
   Includes bibliographical references and index.
   ISBN-13: 978-1-4296-1206-7 (hardcover)
   ISBN-10: 1-4296-1206-1 (hardcover)
   ISBN-13: 978-1-4296-1746-8 (softcover)
   ISBN-10: 1-4296-1746-2 (softcover)
   1. Schools — Juvenile poetry. 2. Children's poetry, American. I. Title. II. Series.
PS3619.A4256D6 2008
811'.6 — dc22   2007029619

Credits
Jenny Marks, editor; Ted Williams, designer; Scott Thoms, photo researcher

Photo Credits
Capstone Press/Karon Dubke, cover, 1, 2–3, 4, 6–7, 8, 10–11, 12, 15, 16–17, 20, 23, 24, 26–27, 28
Getty Images Inc./The Image Bank/Juan Silva, 19; Taxi/Mel Yates, 21; Taxi/Paul Viant, 5

Note to Parents, Teachers, and Librarians
Do Buses Eat Kids?: Poems about School uses colorful photographs and a nonfiction format to introduce children to poetry. This book is designed to be read independently by an early reader or to be read aloud to a pre-reader. The images help early readers and listeners understand the poems and concepts discussed. The book encourages further learning by including the following sections: The Language of Poetry, Glossary, Read More, Internet Sites, and Index. Early readers may need assistance using these features.